Christmas crafting
with kids

catherine woram

photography by
polly wreford

Christmas crafting
with kids   35 projects for the festive season

RYLAND
PETERS
& SMALL
LONDON · NEW YORK

Senior designer Toni Kay
Commissioning editor Annabel Morgan
Picture research Emily Westlake
Production Gemma Moules
Art director Leslie Harrington
Publishing director Alison Starling

Stylist Catherine Woram

First published in the United States in 2008
by Ryland Peters and Small
519 Broadway, 5th Floor
New York, NY 10012
www.rylandpeters.com

10 9 8 7 6 5 4 3 2 1

Text, design and photographs
© Ryland Peters & Small 2008

ISBN: 978-1-84597-700-9

Library of Congress Cataloging-in-Publication Data

Woram, Catherine.
  Christmas crafting with kids : 35 projects for the festive
season / Catherine Woram ; photography by Polly
Wreford.
      p. cm.
  Includes index.
  ISBN 978-1-84597-700-9
  1. Christmas decorations--Juvenile literature. 2.
Handicraft--Juvenile literature. I. Title.
  TT900.C4W664 2008
  745.594'12--dc22
                                2008012958

Printed and bound in China

contents

6 introduction

8 **decorations** pompom tree
decorations * cinnamon sticks * paper
snowflakes * orange tree decorations *
mini tree * paper lanterns * nativity scene *
snow globes * christmas stocking * angel
tree topper * paper chains * clay
decorations * hanging felt stars *
beaded decorations * festive
bells * christmas crackers *
clothespin angel * tealight holders *
gingerbread house * twiggy wreath

70 **gifts** cinnamon cookies * potpourri *
candle centerpiece * glasses case * peppermint
creams * felt egg cozy * button photo frame *
orange pomanders * coconut ice * book bag *
planted bulbs * chocolate brownies * découpaged tin

102 **cards & wrapping** potato print
wrapping paper * stamped gift tags * 3-D christmas
cards * felt motif cards * stenciled gift bag

120 templates
124 sources
126 picture credits
127 index
128 acknowledgments

introduction

If your kids love getting creative with glue, paint, or glitter, or if you enjoyed my previous book, *Crafting with Kids*, then *Christmas Crafting with Kids* is the perfect choice for the festive season and is sure to keep your children busy producing a steady stream of gifts, handmade cards, and decorations. From painted clay stars studded with glitter to jazzy sequined crackers and even a cute Nativity scene, there is something to interest any child, and the wide variety of fun projects will appeal to younger children as well as experienced crafters right up to the age of 11 and beyond. Let your kids go wild exploring their creativity and adding their own personal embellishments to the finished items!

Many traditional crafting techniques are covered here, including potato printing, sewing, painting, and modeling, and there are also several projects that involve cooking—a favorite pastime for most kids. Each project is accompanied by clear and simple step-by-step photographs, and there are also suggestions for other items that can be made employing the same technique. Many projects make use of basic household items such as jelly jars and egg cartons, which is a great way of recycling them—another activity that's sure to appeal to eco-conscious kids.

One of the most rewarding aspects of the creation of this book (as with its predecessor, *Crafting with Kids*) was seeing just how much all the children enjoyed the crafting process. My daughters (Jessica, aged 11, and Anna, aged 9) helped with many of the projects and were a constant source of inspiration. I am sure you will enjoy making the projects in the book just as much as your children will, and that your friends and relatives will delight in receiving them as Christmas cards and gifts, too.

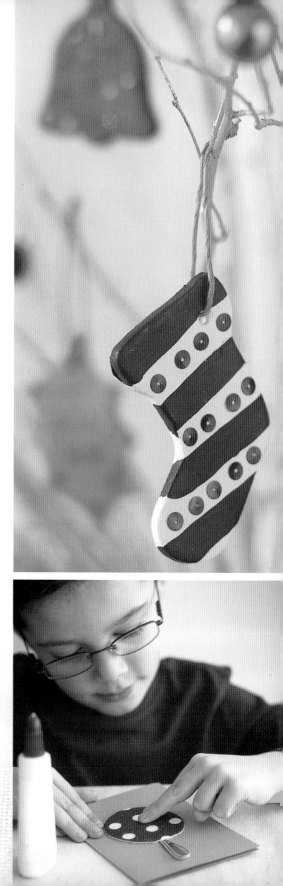

decorations

YOU WILL NEED:

paper • pencil • cardboard • scissors • assorted balls of yarn • 3-D fabric pen in red • approx 4in (10cm) gingham ribbon per ball

wind the yarn

Trace the disk template on page 120 onto paper and cut it out. Place it on a piece of cardboard and draw around it. Repeat. Cut out the two disks. Cut a length of yarn about 2yd (2m) long and wind into a small ball that will fit through the hole in the disks. Start to wind yarn around the disks, binding them together. When the ball of yarn is finished, tie the end to the beginning of a new one. Continue to wind yarn around the disks until they are completely covered.

cut around the outside

When the winding process is complete, hold the pompom disks securely and cut around the edges of the yarn using scissors. The yarn will fall away, looking like fringing at this point, and it is important that the two disks are firmly held together.

secure the yarn

Cut two lengths of yarn about 8in (20cm) long and thread between the two cardboard disks. Pull them together and knot tightly. The loose ends of this yarn will form the hanging loop for the decoration, so tie another knot about 3 in (8cm) from the first knot and neatly trim the ends.

finishing

Gently pull the cardboard disks away from the pompom. If it proves difficult, just cut them off. Trim any excess bits of yarn, and fluff the pompom to give it a nice round shape. Use a 3-D fabric pen to draw tiny dots on the pompom and finish with a length of red gingham ribbon tied in a bow around the hanging loop.

pompom
tree decorations

Pompoms are fun and easy to
make, and you can use them to
create cute Christmas tree balls.
Alternatively, you could make two
different-sized pompoms and glue
them together to make a snowman
or robin, or even a Santa Claus
figure complete with felt hat!

snowmen

Make one small and one large pompom using white yarn and tie the two together using the yarn ends. Trim any uneven ends. Now tie a green pipe cleaner around the snowman's neck to create a scarf, and twist a black pipe cleaner into a hat shape. Glue on a triangle of orange felt for a carrot nose, and use a 3-D fabric pen to draw on his eyes and buttons.

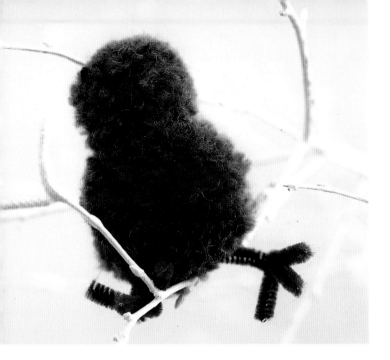

robin tree decoration

Make a small pompom in brown yarn for the head. Now wind red yarn around one half of two larger pompom disks and brown yarn around the other half. Snip around the edges of the disk and secure the pompom with a length of yarn. Use the yarn ends to tie the two pompoms together to form a robin. Add a triangle of red felt for his beak and bend brown pipe cleaners into shape for his feet.

santa claus

Make one large pompom from red yarn for the body. To make the head, wind red yarn around one half of two smaller pompom disks and white yarn around the other half. Snip around the edges of the disk and secure the pompom with a length of yarn. Use the yarn ends to tie the two pompoms together to form a cuddly Santa Claus figure. Add a hat formed from a quarter-circle of red felt, and a black felt belt. Use a black 3-D fabric pen to draw his eyes and buttons.

little tips
Remember: the more yarn you manage to wind around the disks, the fatter your pompom will be. For a really plump pompom, try winding the yarn around the disks twice.

cinnamon sticks

A bundle of cinnamon sticks tied together with red gingham ribbon and finished with a tiny jingle bell makes a pretty and fragrant addition to any Christmas tree.

bundle cinnamon together

Cut an 8in (20cm) length of gingham ribbon. Lay it flat on a table and place five cinnamon sticks on top. Wind the ribbon around the sticks once and pull the ends of the ribbon tight.

YOU WILL NEED
(for each decoration):

five cinnamon sticks • scissors • 16in (40cm) red gingham ribbon, ⅜in (7mm) wide • 2in (5cm) thin wire • small gold bell

arrange ribbon on sticks
Now take the remaining piece of ribbon and lay it on top of the cinnamon sticks, running in the same direction as them, so that the ribbon forms the shape of a cross.

make hanging loop
Bring the two ends of the first piece of ribbon up from beneath the cinnamon sticks, and knot them on top of the sticks. Now make another knot approx 2in (5cm) farther up the ribbon. This will form a loop to hang the decoration from.

finishing
Tie the ends of the second piece of ribbon in a neat bow. Now thread the jingle bell onto the piece of wire, and push the wire through the knot of the bow. Twist the ends of the wire together to secure the bell in place, and trim the wire ends to finish.

YOU WILL NEED:
square pieces of paper •
pencil • scissors

fold paper
Take a square piece of paper. Fold it in half diagonally to form a triangle. Then fold in half again and then into quarters. You should now have a small folded triangle shape.

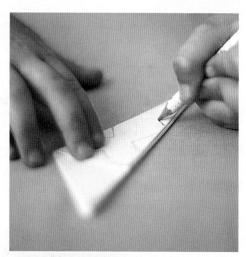

draw on design
Using the pencil, draw triangular or scalloped shapes on the folded edges of the paper. You can draw curved shapes on the top edges of the paper (farthest from the center of the paper), too. Experiment with different shapes, so that all your snowflakes are slightly different.

cut out
Using scissors, carefully cut along the lines you have drawn on the paper. The more shapes you cut out, the more decorative and delicate the finished snowflake will be.

pull open
Gently unfold the paper and carefully press it flat to reveal the snowflake's design. You can cut snowflakes from any piece of paper, but good sizes are an 8in (20cm) square for a large snowflake and a 4in (10cm) square for a small one.

paper snowflakes

Paper snowflakes are so simple to make, yet so
effective. Cut them from white paper, tissue paper
or tracing paper to create pretty and inexpensive
Christmas decorations. They can be used to decorate
windows or suspended from lengths of thread for
a mobile effect. Alternatively, use them to adorn a
vaseful of bare branches for a striking tabletop display.

YOU WILL NEED:
fresh oranges • sharp knife •
dishtowel • paper towels •
cookie sheet • wooden skewer
or awl • 6in (15cm) gingham
ribbon, ½in (10mm) wide, for
each hanging loop

slice the oranges
Ask an adult to cut the orange slices approximately ¼in (5mm) wide. Lay the slices on a dishtowel and blot them with paper towels to remove any excess moisture. This will speed up the drying process.

bake in oven
Lay the orange slices on a metal cookie sheet. Put them in the oven on the lowest setting and leave them for about four hours or until they are completely dry. The trick is to let them "cook" long enough to dry completely. If they do not dry entirely, they won't keep long and may go moldy. Ask an adult to remove the sheet from the oven, as it will be hot.

remove dried oranges
Once the tray has completely cooled, remove the orange slices from the tray and set them aside for decorating. The slices should be hard and dry, but retain their citrus fragrance.

finishing
Ask an adult to make a small hole in the orange using a sharp point such as a wooden skewer. Thread the ribbon through the hole and tie the ends in a knot. Trim the ribbon ends on the diagonal to prevent them from fraying.

orange tree decorations

Dried orange slices hung from a ribbon loop make fragrant and unusual tree decorations. They also make a great addition to our pot-pourri, which can be found on pages 76–77.

mini tree

Use a real or artificial miniature tree to create a fun and festive centerpiece for the Christmas table. Kids will enjoy decorating it with tiny balls, miniature pompoms, and candy canes made from twisted pipe cleaners.

YOU WILL NEED:

miniature Christmas tree • terracotta pot • paintbrushes • undercoat • silver paint • 1yd (1m) gingham ribbon, 1in (2.5cm) wide • scissors • glue • red and white pipe cleaners • 1yd (1m) silver ribbon, ¼in (5mm) wide • red and silver miniature pompoms • 2yd (2m) gingham ribbon, ½in (1cm) wide • miniature balls (if desired)

paint pot Apply a layer of undercoat to the terracotta pot and let it dry completely. Now apply a coat of silver paint and let dry. If necessary, apply a second coat of silver paint for more even coverage, and let it dry.

attach ribbon and bow Measure the circumference of the top of the pot and cut a length of the wider gingham to fit. Glue it around the rim of the pot. Tie a neat bow from the same ribbon and glue it to the front of the pot. Let the glue dry.

make candy canes Twist the bottom ends of the pipe cleaners together so they are attached. Now wind them together for a striped effect.

shape canes Carefully bend one end of the twisted pipe cleaners to form a candy-cane shape with a curved top. Now they can simply be hooked onto the Christmas tree.

make hanging loop Cut a 2½in (6cm) length of the narrow silver ribbon. Fold it in half and pinch the ends together to form a loop. Apply a small dab of glue to hold the ends in place. Let the glue dry.

attach loop Using a pair of scissors, carefully snip open a pompom so that you can see the center. Apply a dab of glue to the middle of the pompom and push in the end of the loop. Press the two sides of the opening closed. Leave the glue to dry completely before hanging the pompoms from the tree.

tie on bows Cut lengths of the narrower gingham ribbon and tie them into bows on the ends of the branches of the Christmas tree. Cut the ends of ribbon on the diagonal to prevent them from fraying.

tie tree topper Cut a 8in (20cm) length of the wider gingham ribbon and tie it around the top of the Christmas tree to make a tree topper, finishing with a pretty bow. Cut the ends on the diagonal to prevent the ribbon fraying.

little tips

The red color scheme we used would work equally well in golds and silvers to create a more luxurious feel for a Christmas table. Or try using all white for an icy winter theme.

YOU WILL NEED:
decorative wrapping paper •
scissors • pencil • ruler • glue •
8in (20cm) sequin trim per
lantern

cut and fold paper
Cut a square of paper measuring 8 by 8in (20 x 20cm) for the lantern and a strip of paper ¾ by 8in (2 by 20cm) for the handle. Fold the square of paper in half and press flat.

clip lantern holes
Take the piece of folded paper and, cutting inward from the folded edge of the paper, use scissors to cut flaps that finish about 1¼in (3cm) from the top of the paper. Each flap should be spaced about ¾in (2cm) apart. You may want to mark the lines using a pencil and a ruler first, to make it easier to cut the paper properly.

glue into round
To make the lantern shape, unfold the paper and roll it to form a tube shape with the paper slits running vertically. Glue the edges of the paper together to form a round tubular lantern, then press downward gently to form a splayed lantern shape.

finishing
Cut a piece of sequin trim to fit around the top of the lantern and glue it in place. Glue the ends of the hanging loop to the inside of the lantern on both sides and let dry completely.

paper lanterns

Paper lanterns are a traditional and fun way of using a piece of paper to make three-dimensional objects. They look very pretty fashioned from soft pink and silver wrapping paper and trimmed with sequins for a festive look. They would also look great in simple red and white trimmed with patterned ribbon.

nativity scene

A wonderful family keepsake that can be
brought out every year, this Nativity scene
is made from Fimo colored modeling
clay. Each figure is based
on a simple tube shape
and decorated with
touches of gold.

YOU WILL NEED:

Fimo modeling clay in assorted colors • small rolling pin • raffia for crib • scissors • Fimo gold dust for decorating • paintbrush

make baby Take some white modeling clay and roll out a bean shape about 1¼in (3cm) in length for the baby's body. If the clay is hard, work it between the hands to soften it, so it is easier to mold into shape.

make face Take a small piece of flesh-colored clay and roll it into a ball. Flatten it with your fingers to form a small round disk. Press the disk firmly onto the top of the body shape. Use tiny pieces of black clay to make the eyes and a mouth, and press them in position on the face.

make crib Take the brown clay and roll it into a bean shape about 1½in (4cm) in length and about ¾in (2cm) in diameter. Use your thumb to press down and make an indentation in the crib. Roll two balls of brown modeling clay and press them flat to make the legs of the crib.

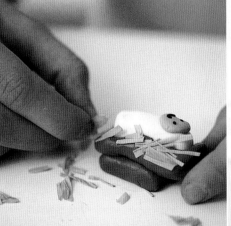

decorate with raffia Use scissors to snip small pieces of raffia for the straw in the crib. Press the pieces of raffia firmly against the sides of the crib until they stick in place.

make other figures Each figure for the Nativity scene is made from a basic bean shape formed from clay and measuring approximately 2in (5cm) in length and ¾in (2cm) in diameter. Take a small piece of flesh-colored clay, roll it in a ball, and press it flat to form the face. Using the same method, make a beard from brown clay and use tiny pieces of black clay for the eyes and mouth.

make cloaks To make the cloak, roll out a piece of clay to approximately 4in (10cm) long by ½in (1cm) wide. Fold it over the body and press firmly in place. If the cloak is too long, trim the ends with scissors.

attach arms Make two small rolls of flesh-colored clay for the arms and press them firmly against the front of the body. Use more small pieces of clay to form the gifts for the Wise Men to carry, and press them in position between the arms at the front of the body.

finishing The Wise Men's gifts and crowns are finished with fine gold dust applied with a paintbrush. Lay the figure on its side while you apply the dust, to prevent it from falling on the rest of the figure.

snow globes

Snow globes make great gifts for friends and family, and children really enjoy making them.

YOU WILL NEED:

empty, clean glass jars with lids • silver paint • paintbrush • waterproof glue or tile adhesive • Christmas decorations to put in jar • jug and spoon for pouring • distilled water • glycerin • clear dishwashing detergent • glitter

paint lid
You may wish to sand the metal lid lightly before painting. Paint the lid of the jar with silver paint and let it dry completely. If required, apply a second coat of paint for better coverage and again leave to dry.

attach decoration
Use strong glue to attach the decoration to the inside of the jar lid. If the decoration is on the small side, build up a small mound using waterproof tile adhesive and press the decoration firmly into it. Leave until completely dry.

fill jar and add glitter
Use a jug to pour the distilled water into the jar. Fill it right up to the brim. Now stir in two teaspoons of glycerin and half a teaspoon of detergent. Add five or six spoonfuls of glitter to the water. White or silver glitter looks most similar to snow, although bright colors like red or green can look very jolly and festive.

finishing
Carefully place the lid on the top of the jar and screw the lid tightly in place. The jar should be watertight, but you may wish to seal it around the edges with a thin layer of silicone sealant, which is available from craft stores.

christmas stocking

Create this pretty Shaker-style
stocking in cream wool and
decorate with a simple heart
and mother-of-pearl button.
You could make one for each
member of the family and
tie on card name tags.

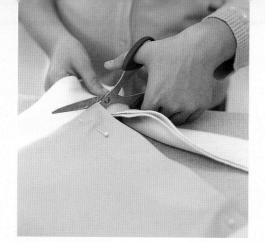

YOU WILL NEED:

paper • pencil • scissors • 16in (40cm) cream wool fabric, 44in (137cm) wide • pins • 6 x 6in (15 x 15cm) red felt for heart motif • needle • white thread • red thread • glue • pearl button • red embroidery thread • 8in (20cm) gingham fabric, 44in (137cm) wide • 4in (10cm) gingham ribbon

create a template
Trace the stocking template on page 123 onto a piece of paper. Now enlarge it on a photocopier at 200% to make it the right size. Cut out the template. Fold the cream wool fabric in half and pin the template to the fabric. Cut out the stocking pieces.

cut out heart motif
Trace the heart template on page 123 on a piece of paper and cut it out. Pin the template to the felt and cut out a heart to decorate the front of the stocking.

baste heart to stocking
Thread the needle with white thread and baste the heart motif to the front stocking piece.

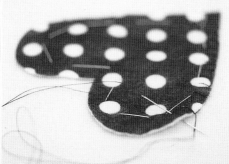

blanket-stitch heart
Now thread the needle with red thread and work small blanket stitches all the way around the heart motif. When you have finished, remove the basting. Now use a dab of glue to stick the pearl button to the center of the heart.

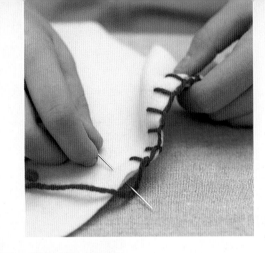

stitch stocking together

With right sides together, baste the two stocking pieces together. Turn right side out. Thread a needle with the red embroidery thread and work blanket stitch all the way around the edges of the stocking, leaving the straight top edges of the stocking open. Press flat using a warm iron (it is advisable for an adult to do this).

make gingham border

Fold the piece of gingham fabric in half lengthwise, right sides together, and stitch the side seams together using small running stitches. Turn right side out and press flat using an iron (it is advisable for an adult to do this).

stitch gingham to stocking

Turn a ½in (1cm) hem to the inside of the gingham and press flat. Tuck about 3in (8cm) of the gingham fabric inside the stocking and fold the remainder of the fabric over the top of the stocking, with the hemmed edge on the outside. Sew small running stitches all around the top of the gingham fabric to hold it in place.

sew on hanging loop

Fold the piece of gingham ribbon in half to form a loop, and stitch it to the inside of the gingham fabric at the back seam of the stocking.

little tips

The stocking would work equally well in a bright Christmassy red color. Other jolly variations would be a star or Christmas tree motif on the front of the stocking. Alternatively, you could write the child's name using a 3-D fabric pen.

angel
tree topper

Decorate simple cones
of card with a sprinkling of
glitter and a pompom to
create pretty tree-top angels
complete with silver pipe
cleaner or feather wings.

YOU WILL NEED:

10in (25cm) diameter plate as template for cone shape • silver card • pencil • scissors • glue • silver glitter • stapler • silver pipe cleaner • pompom for head • blue and pink 3-D fabric pens for face • gold pipe cleaner

draw around plate Place the plate on the silver card and draw around half of it to create a semicircle for the cone. Cut out.

apply glitter Use glue to draw a scalloped line all around the curved edge of the semicircular piece of card. Sprinkle silver glitter over the glue and leave for a few minutes. Shake off any excess glitter and let the glue dry completely.

form cone shape Form the card semicircle into a cone shape (folding it gently in half and making a slight crease at the center of the card makes it a bit easier to form a cone). Use a stapler to join the card together.

make wings Use the silver pipe cleaner to form the wings. Twist the ends over to form a figure eight.

attach wings Apply a dab of glue to the center of the wings and glue them to the back of the cone, about 1¼in (3cm) down from the top. Allow glue to dry completely.

glue on pompom head Use a readymade pompom or make your own following the instructions on pages 10–11. Glue the pompom to the top of the cone and leave to dry.

draw face Use 3-D fabric pens in pink and blue to draw the angel's eyes and mouth on the pompom. Leave to dry.

finishing For a halo, bend a gold pipe cleaner into a circular shape with a diameter of about 1¼in (3cm). Twist the ends together to secure, and glue it to the top of the pompom head to finish.

little tips

Use red card to make a Santa Claus tree topper complete with a cotton beard or a Rudolf the Reindeer tree topper using brown card and a pair of pipe-cleaner antlers!

paper chains

Traditional paper chains are easy to make and look great
made in festive paper for Christmas. We used decorative gold
and silver patterned wrapping paper, but they would work
equally well in red and white
or even icy blues and
silver tones.

YOU WILL NEED:
scissors • gold and silver wrapping paper • pencil • ruler • glue • stapler (if desired)

draw lines on paper Cut the wrapping paper into pieces that are at least 8in (20cm) long. Using a pencil and ruler, draw lines on the back of the paper, making sure that each one is approximately ¾in (2cm) wide. Repeat with the different colored paper.

cut out strips Use the scissors to cut out the paper strips. It is a good idea to keep the colors separate by making a pile of strips in each color, so they are easier to select when making the chain.

form first link Bend the paper to form a loop and apply a dab of glue to hold it together. Press flat and allow glue to dry. You can use a stapler instead of glue, which is quicker, but the staples will be visible.

continue making chain Thread the end of a second paper strip through the first loop and glue the ends together. Continue threading alternate strips of silver and gold paper until you have made the required length of paper chain.

YOU WILL NEED:

air-drying modeling clay • rolling pin • snowflake-shaped cookie cutter • drinking straw (for piercing hole) • spatula • paints in desired colors • saucer for paint • paintbrushes • glue • glitter • ribbon for hanging loop, ¼in (5mm) wide

roll out clay Remove the clay from its packaging and knead to soften it. Roll the clay out with a rolling pin. For smaller snowflakes, the clay should be about ¼in (5mm) thick. For larger snowflakes, the clay should be about ½in (1cm) thick.

cut out shape Use the snowflake cookie cutter to cut the shape from the clay. Carefully remove the excess clay from around the cutter before lifting it off. Use the end of a drinking straw to pierce a ribbon hole to hang the snowflake from. Use a spatula to lift the clay shape and place it on a tray to dry. When the top is dry, turn the shape over so the other side can dry completely, too. This prevents the edges from curling as the clay dries.

paint and decorate Apply a coat of white paint to the top and sides of each snowflake and allow to dry completely. When dry, paint the other side. Leave to dry. If necessary, apply a further coat of paint for better coverage.

finishing Apply dots of glue to the front of the decoration and then sprinkle silver glitter over the snowflake. Gently shake off the glitter onto a plate, and leave to dry. Cut a 3in (8cm) length of ribbon and thread through the hole in the snowflake. Knot the ends to form a hanging loop for the decoration.

clay decorations

Children love working with clay, and it can be used to create fun festive-shaped decorations that are painted and decorated with glitter, then threaded on ribbon to hang from the tree. Other Christmas cookie cutters can be used to make more decorations, as shown overleaf.

festive shapes

Bright, bold red, green, and white paint gives these simple shapes their punchy effect. They were made with holly-, bell- and stocking-shaped cookie cutters and decorated with single sequins attached with a dot of glue. Colored string was used to hang them from the branches.

star gift tag

Use a small star-shaped cookie cutter to make a cute decorative gift tag. Remember to pierce a hole using a drinking straw then, when the clay is dry, paint both sides of the star with silver paint. We used frosty sheer white ribbon to tie the star to the gift.

little tips
Avoid putting the clay near water, as it will make it sticky and difficult to use. Keep left-over clay wrapped in plastic in an airtight container for future use. A couple of coats of water-based varnish (applied by an adult) will give the painted clay a longer life.

hanging felt stars

Cut from red and green felt using pinking shears, these jolly tree decorations are an ideal easy sewing project for little fingers. We decorated the star shapes with pretty buttons and hung them from rickrack loops.

YOU WILL NEED:

paper • pencil • scissors • colored felt • pins • pinking shears • 6in (15cm) red rickrack per decoration • matching cotton thread • needle • polyester stuffing • glue • assorted pearl buttons (approx 8 per decoration)

make template Trace the star template on page 120 onto paper and cut it out.

draw around template Fold the felt in half, as you will need two star shapes per decoration. Use a pencil to draw around the star motif on the felt fabric (it may be easier if you first pin the star motif to the felt to keep it in place).

cut out Using pinking shears, carefully cut all the way around the star shape, making sure you are cutting through both layers of fabric. The pinking shears give an attractive zigzag effect to the edges and, if you are using cotton or linen, will prevent the fabric from fraying. If you are making more than one star decoration, it is a good idea to cut them all out at one time.

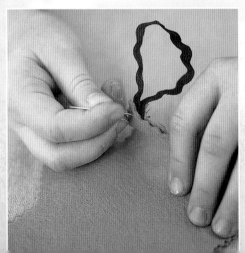

attach loop Fold a 6in (15cm) length of rickrack in half and place between the two layers of felt at the top of one of the points. Thread the needle. Push the needle through the two layers of felt, sandwiching the loop between them, and make two or three stitches to secure the hanging loop.

little tips

Use different shapes such as hearts and fill with dried lavender to make cute scented gifts for your family and friends. Sequins or beads can be used instead of buttons for a more festive look.

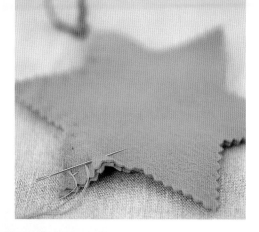

stitch together Continue stitching all the way around the points of the star, using small running stitches about ¼in (3mm) from the edge. Stitch around five sides of the star, but leave the sixth side open for the stuffing.

stuff heart Carefully push the stuffing into the opening. You may need to use the end of a knitting needle or a pencil to make sure that the stuffing is right down inside all the points of the star.

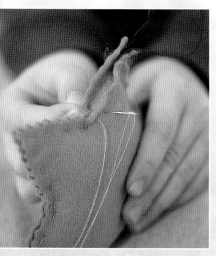

stitch opening closed Hold the two layers of felt together and stitch the opening closed, using the same small running stitches about ¼in (3mm) from the edges of the fabric. Tie off the stitching by making two or three stitches together, and snip the loose ends of the thread.

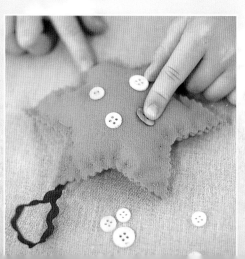

finishing Use dabs of glue to stick the buttons to the front of the star decoration and leave to dry completely. You may wish to glue buttons to the other side of the decoration if they are to be hung on a tree, and you will need extra buttons for this.

YOU WILL NEED:
12in (30cm) wire per heart •
glass rocaille beads • pliers
(if required) • silver ribbon,
¼in (5mm) wide • scissors

thread beads on wire Fold the
wire in half and bend it into a "V" shape
to form the base of the heart. Begin
threading beads onto both sides of the
wire. Continue threading until all the wire
is covered, only leaving about ¾in (2cm)
of bare wire at each end.

shape into heart Hold the ends of the wire and bend
them inward to form the curved top of the heart. Twist the
ends together to prevent the beads from falling off the wire.

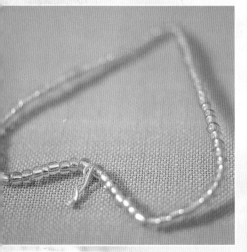

twist ends of wire Twist the ends of the wire to form a loop for
the ribbon. If the wire is very stiff, it may be advisable for an adult to do
this, using a pair of pliers.

attach hanging loop and bow
Cut a 4in (10cm) length of ribbon. Thread
it through the wire and knot the ends of
the ribbon to form a loop. Trim the ends
of the ribbon on the diagonal to prevent
them fraying. Cut another length of ribbon
about 4in (10cm) in length and tie around
the wire in a pretty bow to finish.

beaded decorations

These dainty Christmas tree decorations are
fashioned from fine wire threaded with tiny
glass rocaille beads and bent into the shape
of a heart. They would look good all year
round hung from wall hooks or a doorknob.

YOU WILL NEED:

a cardboard egg carton • scissors • pencil • gold and silver paint • paintbrush • glue • gold and silver glitter • awl or wooden skewer • small jingle bells • 8in (20cm) gold or silver cord

cut out bells   Use scissors to cut the cups from the egg carton. Use a pencil to draw a decorative scalloped line around the bottom edges and cut out, following the line. You could also try cutting the ends with pinking shears for a decorative zigzag effect.

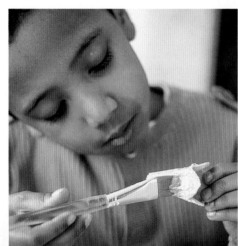

paint bells   Paint the bells both inside and out and leave to dry. You will need to apply a second coat, as the cardboard will absorb a lot of the paint. Leave the paint to dry completely.

decorate with glitter   Apply dabs of glue all the way around the bottom of each bell. Sprinkle glitter onto the glue and shake off any excess onto a plate. Leave the glue to dry completely.

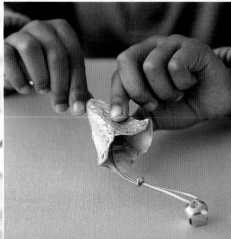

thread bell   Using an awl, pierce a hole in the top of the bell (it is advisable for an adult to do this). Cut an 8in (20cm) length of cord and thread the bell onto it. Make a knot about 2in (5cm) up from the bell, then thread the ends of the cord through the hole in the top of the bell. Tie a knot at the top of the cord to finish.

festive bells

These festive bells are made from cardboard egg cartons, which give them their bell-like shape. To finish, they were painted silver and gold and decorated with glitter.

christmas crackers

Making your own crackers is fun and easy, and it means you can put your own choice of novelties and silly handwritten jokes inside. Make the crackers from colorful wrapping paper and trim them with sequins or glitter finished with pretty bows.

YOU WILL NEED:

cardboard toilet rolls • 8 x 12in (20 x 30cm) piece of paper per cracker • pencil • ruler • scissors • glue or tape • snaps for cracker • gifts, paper hats, and jokes • 8in (20cm) ribbon, ¼in (5mm) wide, per cracker • sequin trim

mark paper Lay the cardboard roll in the center of the paper and mark the position of each end using a pencil. Set the roll aside.

draw lines Using the marks made on the paper as a guide, fold the paper in, right sides together, and press the folds flat. Using a ruler, mark lines along the paper about ¾in (2cm) apart, starting about 1in (2.5cm) in from the outside edge of the paper.

cut slits Use scissors to cut along the marked lines to create slits in the paper. Repeat on the other side. These slits enable the cracker ends to be tied more easily.

roll cracker Now unfold the paper and lay it flat. Place the cardboard roll on top. Apply a dab of glue or use a small piece of tape to hold the paper on the roll. Wrap the paper around the roll as tightly as you can.

glue paper to roll Apply glue along the whole edge of the paper and press firmly in place. Allow the glue to dry completely.

insert snap Push the cracker snap through the open end of the roll. This is also the time to insert any small gifts or trinkets, a paper hat, and a joke or other motto.

tie on ribbon Gently tie a 4in (10cm) length of ribbon around one end of the cracker. Tie in a knot. Repeat at the other end. Trim the ends of the ribbon on the diagonal with scissors, to prevent them from fraying.

finishing Measure the circumference of the cracker and cut three lengths of sequin trim to fit. Glue the sequin trim in rows around the cracker. Allow glue to dry completely.

YOU WILL NEED:
pencil • paper • scissors • wooden clothespin • white, silver, and yellow paint • fine paintbrush • black pen • a paper doily • glue • silver card • silver pipe cleaner • sheer ribbon

make template Trace the angel wing template on page 121 onto paper and cut it out.

paint body Paint the body of the clothespin white (this prevents the wood from showing through the holes in the doily). Leave the head unpainted. Paint the tips of the clothespin silver (for the angel's feet) and allow to dry completely.

draw on face Use the yellow paint to give the angel hair, and allow to dry completely. You may need to apply a second coat of paint for better coverage. Use the black pen to draw two eyes and a mouth.

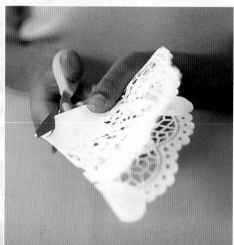

make robes Fold the paper doily in half and cut along the folded edge. Fold one half of the doily in half again and cut a small quarter-circle from the corner to fit around the neck of the clothespin.

clothespin angel

Clothespin dolls make perfect
Christmas decorations dressed
as angels and hung from the
tree. They also look cute
dressed up as Santa
Claus and wrapped
in red felt with a
cotton beard!

glue on dress Wrap the doily around the doll and apply a dab of glue at the back of the neck to hold it in place. Now glue all the way along the back of the dress from top to bottom, then leave to dry completely.

cut out wings Use a pencil to draw around the paper wing template on the back of the silver card. Cut the wings out and apply a dab of the glue to the center of the silver side of the card.

glue on wings Press the wings onto the back of the peg-doll angel, approximately ½ in (1cm) below the neck. Allow the glue to dry completely.

finishing Wrap the silver pipe cleaner around the angel's head to calculate the length required for the halo. Bend the pipe cleaner into a circular halo and twist the ends together. Place on the angel's head and glue in place. Tie a length of ribbon around the neck and knot the ends to form a hanging loop.

tealight holders

Plain glass tealight holders have been decorated with simple snowflake motifs to create pretty decorations that would make welcome gifts for family and friends. Fill with scented tealights to finish.

YOU WILL NEED:
pencil • paper • scissors • masking tape • glass tealight holders • 3-D fabric pens

draw motif Trace the snowflake motif on page 123 onto paper. Cut the paper into a small square that will fit inside the tealight holder.

place motif in glass Place the paper motif inside the glass tealight holder and use small pieces of masking tape to hold it in place. The design should face outward so it is clearly visible through the glass of the holder.

fill in motif Starting from the center, using a 3-D fabric pen, draw small dots approximately ⅛in (2mm) apart all the way along the lines of the snowflake stencil. Be careful not to smudge the paint as you work – it takes about an hour to dry completely.

finishing Continue filling in the dots along the lines of the stencil, then allow the paint to dry completely. You could experiment with other patterns, such as a simple row of dots around the rim of the tealight holder. When the paint has dried, drop a colored or scented tealight inside each holder.

gingerbread house

This decorative gingerbread house makes a fabulous table centerpiece for Christmas and will elicit "oohs" and "aahs" of admiration when it's unveiled! We decorated the plain gingerbread with white frosting, candy, and candy canes, as well as silver sugar balls.

YOU WILL NEED:

5 cookie sheets • baking parchment • 1 cup (225g) all-purpose flour, plus extra for dusting • 1 tsp ground ginger • 1 tsp ground cinnamon • 1 tsp baking soda • 4 tbsp butter • 2 tbsp dark brown sugar • ⅓ cup (80g) dark cane syrup • 1 tbsp beaten egg • rolling pin • foil cake board • confectioner's sugar • silver balls • tubes of icing • 2 red gumdrops • rock candy canes • small red and white candies to decorate

mix ingredients
Preheat the oven to 375°F (190°C) and cover five cookie sheets with baking parchment. Now sift the flour, ginger, cinnamon, and baking soda into the bowl of an electric mixer or a food processor. Add the butter and mix until the mixture resembles fine breadcrumbs.

add sugar and syrup
Now add the brown sugar, cane syrup, and egg to the mixer bowl and blitz to form a soft dough. If the consistency is too dry, add a little more egg.

roll out the dough
Roll the dough out to a ½ in (1cm) thickness, so that it is firm enough to hold its shape when cooked. Cut out two large rectangles for the roof, two smaller rectangular side panels, and a front and back section with a pointed gable. Use the template on page 122 for the front and back section.

place on cookie sheet
Carefully lay the pieces of the gingerbread house on separate cookie sheets. Bake for 8–10 minutes until a light golden brown in color. Leave on the cookie sheets until firm to the touch, then transfer to a rack to cool.

build the house
Make some frosting following the instructions on the box. The consistency should be thick enough to "glue" the gingerbread together. Spread frosting along the front of the cake board and stand the front section of the house on top. When it is stable, apply more frosting to one end of the side walls and stick them to the front section. Hold the two pieces in place until secure. Now attach the back section to the other ends of the walls. Let the frosting dry completely.

decorate the roof
Use a ready-mixed tube of frosting to pipe a scalloped tiled pattern to the roof. Decorate the frosting with silver balls and let dry completely. Repeat for the other section of the roof, and let dry.

finishing
Pipe on the windows using the tube of frosting. Pipe a door shape on the front section, then stick hard candy to the frosting. Use frosting to attach candy around the edges of the house. Apply more frosting to the edges of the house, and carefully place the roof in position. Hold in place until the frosting holds (or use cocktail sticks to support it from beneath). When the frosting is completely dry, decorate the roof ridge with hard candy and add two gumdrops as chimneys.

little tips

Try using any left-over gingerbread mixture to make tiny gingerbread figures to place outside the house. You can decorate them with icing to create cute Santa figures, cheery snowmen, or jolly reindeer!

twiggy wreath

Make this decorative door wreath from natural twigs and decorate with dried leaves painted silver and gold. Hang it on the front door, or lay it flat on a table and fill the center with candles for a striking table decoration.

YOU WILL NEED:

assortment of natural-colored twigs • 10in (25cm) diameter florist's wire ring • string • scissors • dried leaves in assorted shapes • gold and silver paint • paintbrush • glue • 18in (50cm) gold ribbon, 1¼in (3cm) wide, for bow

tie on twigs Carefully bend the twigs in place around the wire ring and use short lengths of string to tie them in place. Continue until the wire ring is completely covered with and concealed by the twigs. Trim any very long twigs with scissors.

paint leaves Lay the dried leaves facing up on a large piece of paper and paint each one with gold or silver paint. Let them dry thoroughly and apply a further coat to each leaf if better coverage is required.

glue on leaves Apply three or four dabs of glue to the back of a leaf and stick it to the twigs. Continue to glue on the leaves, placing them at regular intervals and alternating between silver and gold, until the wreath is covered with a layer of painted leaves.

finishing Tie the length of gold ribbon at the top of the wreath and make a bow. Trim the ends of the ribbon on the diagonal to prevent them from fraying.

gifts

cinnamon cookies

These yummy cookies decorated with icing and silver balls make perfect gifts for teachers, neighbors, or other grown-ups. You could also hang them from lengths of festive ribbon to make pretty tree decorations.

YOU WILL NEED:

1 cup (225g) all-purpose flour, plus extra for dusting • 1 tsp ground cinnamon • 1 tsp ground ginger • 1tsp baking soda • 4 tbsps butter • 2 tbsps dark brown sugar • ⅓ cup (80g) dark cane syrup syrup • 1tbsp beaten egg • rolling pin • star-shaped cookie cutter • drinking straw • baking tray • confectioner's sugar, silver balls, and other decorations of your choice • narrow ribbon

MAKES 25 SMALL COOKIES

get started Preheat the oven to 375°F (190°C). Cover two cookie sheets with baking parchment.

add the flour Sift the flour, cinnamon, ginger, and baking soda into a wide bowl or food processor. Add the butter and mix with a wooden spoon or whizz in the processor until the mixture resembles fine breadcrumbs.

form dough Add the sugar, cane syrup, and egg and mix together or whizz in the food processor to make a soft dough. If it feels too dry, add a little more egg. Now form the dough into a ball, then flatten it ready for rolling.

roll out dough Using a rolling pin, carefully and evenly roll out the dough to a thickness of about ¼in (5mm).

cut out cookies Using star-shaped cookie cutters, cut out the cookies. Use a drinking straw to punch a small hanging hole in each cookie, about ½ in (1cm) from the edge. Place the cookies on the cookie sheet. Bake them in the oven for 8–10 minutes until light golden brown.

make frosting Leave the baked cookies on the trays until they are firm, then transfer to a rack to cool. To decorate the cookies, you can either use ready-mixed frosting, which is available in tubes and bottles, or make your own by beating together confectioner's sugar and water to create a thin frosting (you can add food coloring for more colorful effects).

decorate cookies Use the frosting to decorate the cookies, then add more decorations. Silver and gold sugar balls look suitably festive on Christmas cookies, and you can try adding colored sugar and other pretty sprinkles, too.

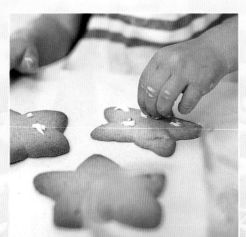

finishing Once the decorations have dried completely, thread a length of narrow ribbon through the hole in each cookie. If you can resist eating them, they are now ready to be boxed up as gifts or hung from the Christmas tree!

YOU WILL NEED:

pine cones, cinnamon sticks and dried
orange slices (see pages 18–19) •
cellophane bags • air-drying clay • small
heart-shaped cookie cutter • drinking
straw • green paint • paintbrush • 8in
(20cm) narrow gingham ribbon, ½in (1cm)
wide • 12in (30cm) gingham ribbon, ¾in
(2cm) wide

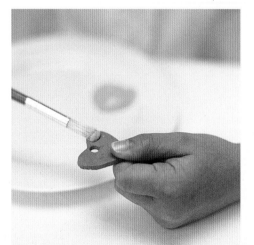

fill bag Make the dried orange slices following the instructions on page 18–19. Put the cones, cinnamon sticks, and orange slices into a bowl. Now fill the cellophane bag with the potpourri, layering the different items for an attractive effect.

paint clay decorations Following the instructions on page 42-43, make two clay hearts per bag of potpourri. Use a heart-shaped cookie cutter to cut them out, and use a drinking straw to pierce a hole in each one to thread the ribbon through. Let dry, then paint the hearts green on both sides.

tie on clay decorations Thread the narrow ribbon through the holes of one heart and tie a knot at the back to prevent it from slipping off. Tie the narrow ribbon around the neck of the bag and pull tight. Now tie the wider ribbon together around the ends of the narrow ribbon, just below the knot.

finishing Tie the wider ribbon in a bow around the cellophane. Tease up the top of the cellophane bag so that it sticks out attractively. Trim the ends of the ribbon on the diagonal to prevent the ends from fraying.

potpourri

Potpourri is fun and easy to make and is always
a welcome gift. It looks very pretty wrapped in a
glossy cellophane bag and decorated with ribbon
and heart-shaped clay decorations.

candle centerpiece

A simple terracotta flowerpot painted silver, decorated with ivy leaves and holding a simple pillar candle makes a simple yet effective centerpiece for the Christmas table. Group them together in a row of three for a more dramatic effect.

YOU WILL NEED:
terracotta flowerpot, 6in (15cm)
diameter • undercoat • silver
paint • paintbrushes • double-
sided tape • 18in (50cm) sheer
silver ribbon, 1in (2.5cm) wide •
pillar candle, approx 8in (20cm)
tall • sand or fine gravel • fresh
or artificial ivy leaves

paint flowerpot Apply a coat of
undercoat to the terracotta pot and leave
to dry completely. Now apply a coat of
silver paint and let dry. Paint the inside
of the pot and leave to dry. If necessary,
apply a further coat of paint for better
coverage, then allow to dry completely.

tie on bow Place a small piece of double-sided tape at the
back of the pot on the rim and press the center of the ribbon to
it, so it is securely fixed in place. Tie the ribbon into a decorative
bow at the front of the pot. Trim the ends of the ribbon on the
diagonal to prevent the ends from fraying.

add candle Place the candle in the terracotta pot. If it is slightly wobbly,
you may find it easier to put some sand or fine gravel in the bottom of the pot
to support the candle and hold it in place. Remember to cover the hole in the
base of the pot with a piece of tape first!

finishing Use fresh or artificial ivy
leaves to decorate the rim of the pot.
You will need to use a dab of glue to
hold them in place. If the pot is intended
as a gift, it is better to use artificial
leaves, as they will last longer.

YOU WILL NEED:

paper • pencil • scissors •
colored felt, 12in (30cm) square •
pins • pinking shears • needle •
embroidery floss • 8in (20cm)
rickrack or braid • glue

create a template Trace the glasses case template on page 122 on paper and cut it out. Fold the felt in half, with right sides together, place the paper template on the wrong side of the felt, and draw all the way around the template using a pencil. It may be easier if you pin the template to the felt before you draw around it.

cut out fabric Firmly holding the two layers of felt together, use pinking shears to cut out the glasses case. Do not cut along the top straight edge of the case.

stitch pieces together Thread a needle with the embroidery thread and, with wrong sides of the fabric together, use simple running stitch of about ½in (1cm) length to sew all the way around the outside edge of the case. Leave the top straight edge of the glasses case open.

finishing Take the length of rickrack and place one end at the center back of the glasses case, approximately ¾in (2cm) below the open edge. Apply a thin line of glue to the back of the rickrack, and press down to attach it to the glasses case. Leave the glue to dry completely.

glasses case

A great gift for grandparents, this fun glasses case is quick and easy to make from polka-dot felt and rickrack in jolly colors.

YOU WILL NEED:

1lb (500g) confectioner's sugar •
4 tbsps condensed milk • oil of
peppermint • miniature silver
petit-four cases • pale blue
ready-rolled icing • ready-mixed
tubes of black and brown icing

MAKES 16 SNOWMEN

mix ingredients Sift the sugar into a bowl and stir in the condensed milk until the mixture becomes a smooth paste. Add three drops of oil of peppermint and knead it into the mixture until the flavor is thoroughly worked through. Add more oil of peppermint a drop at a time and knead it in thoroughly until you achieve the desired flavor.

form snowmen Roll the mixture between the palms of your hands to form the ball for the bottom half of the snowman. Place in a silver petit-four case and then roll a smaller ball for the head. Place the head gently on top of the larger ball and push down to secure.

add scarves Roll out the pale blue icing. Ask an adult to use a sharp knife to cut lengths measuring about ¼in (5mm) wide by 4in (10cm) long. Wrap one around the neck of each snowman to form a scarf.

finishing Use ready-mixed black icing to form the snowmen's hats and eyes. To finish, roll blobs of brown icing into tiny balls for the snowmen's noses and stick them firmly in place. Let the snowmen dry completely before packaging them.

peppermint creams

Delicious to eat and oh-so-easy to make, peppermint creams make great gifts, and the mixture can be used to form fun shapes, such as these cute snowmen with their black icing hats and cozy blue scarves!

felt egg cozy

This cute, colorful felt egg cozy is easy
to create and makes a great gift. Younger
children who are not quite as proficient
at sewing may need some
help with the stitching.
You can also use glue
to attach the motif
shape to the cozy.

YOU WILL NEED:

paper • pencil • pins • scissors •
felt in two different colors •
cookie cutters to use as
stencils for motifs • sewing
thread in two different colors •
needle • glue • pretty buttons
to decorate

create template
Trace the egg cozy template on page 121 onto a piece of plain paper and cut it out. Pin the template to the fabric and cut out two shapes. Now use a cookie cutter to cut out a star (or tree) motif from the different-colored felt.

stitch on motif
Using small blanket stitches in contrasting thread, stitch the felt motif to the front of one of the the egg cozy pieces. Use two strands of thread to make the stitches more visible. Younger children may find it easier to glue the motif to the egg cozy.

stitch together
Place the two egg cozy pieces with right sides together. Stitch the back and front of the egg cozy together using blanket stitch. When you have finished stitching around the sides, continue the blanket stitch along the two open bottom edges of the egg cozy.

finishing
Decorate the felt motifs using pretty mother-of-pearl buttons. Use a small dab of glue on the back of each button and stick it to the felt motif to finish.

YOU WILL NEED:

plain wood picture frame • red or green paint • paintbrushes • assorted red buttons in different shapes and sizes, but approx ⅜in (1cm) in diameter • glue • colored pencils • paper

paint frame   Paint the wooden frame using your chosen color of paint and let it dry completely. If necessary, apply a further coat of paint for better coverage, then allow to dry completely.

glue buttons to corners   Glue a button to each corner of the frame and press down firmly to make sure that they are firmly stuck in place. You may wish to use buttons in an assortment of bright colors. Alternatively, mother-of-pearl buttons can look very pretty.

continue to glue on buttons   Continue to glue on the rest of the buttons, working all the way around the frame and alternating different sizes and shapes. Press down hard on each button as you glue it in place to make sure that it is secure. Leave to dry completely.

draw pictures   Use colored pencils to draw a festive picture to insert in the finished frame—Christmas trees, stars, bells, or Santas would all look great.

button photo frame

Painted in festive red and green and decorated with jolly buttons, this fun photo frame makes a great gift for a granny or grandpa, especially when used to display children's own artwork.

orange pomanders

These traditional pomanders made from oranges and decorated with cloves have long been associated with Christmas. Their sweet, spicy smell makes them welcome gifts for family and friends, or pretty decorations to hang in the home.

YOU WILL NEED:
ballpoint pen • large orange •
awl (for piercing holes) • cloves •
15in (60cm) ribbon, ½in (1cm)
wide • scissors • pin

mark ribbon positions Use
the pen to mark the ribbon positions
around the orange. The ribbon is wrapped
around the orange in the shape of a cross.
Use the awl to pierce holes for the cloves
on the four quarters of the orange. Awls
are very sharp, so it is advisable for an
adult to pierce the holes.

insert cloves Carefully push the cloves into the orange.
The tops of the cloves tend to be quite brittle, so push them
in gently. Continue to push the cloves into the orange until
all four quarters are covered.

anchor ribbon Wrap a length of ribbon around the orange so the ends
overlap at the bottom of the orange. Snip the ribbon and hold the first piece in
place as you wrap another length around the orange. Trim any trailing ribbon
ends. Now push a pin through the ends of the ribbon to hold it in place.

finishing Thread a length of ribbon
through the top of the crossed ribbon
on the orange and tie the ends together.
Tie a knot in the ribbon about 2in (5cm)
from the top of the orange to form a
loop. Now thread a further length of
ribbon through the top of the ribbon
and tie into a pretty bow to finish.

YOU WILL NEED:

1½lbs (750g) confectioner's sugar, sifted • 1 cup (250ml) canned sweetened condensed milk • ¾ cup (375g) desiccated coconut • 2 tbsps freshly squeezed lemon juice • 3-4 drops vanilla essence • 5–6 drops pink food coloring • rolling pin • cookie sheet, 7 x 11in (28 x 18cm), lined with baking parchment and dusted with confectioner's sugar • cookie cutters in festive shapes • sifter

MAKES ABOUT 40 PIECES OR 10 BARS

mix ingredients Put the sifted sugar in a large bowl, add the condensed milk, and mix with a wooden spoon until smooth. Add the coconut, lemon juice, and vanilla, and stir to form a stiff paste. Add the pink food coloring and mix well until the color is evenly worked through.

roll out mixture Let the mixture set for about half an hour so that it becomes firmer. Sprinkle the rolling surface with confectioner's sugar and roll out the mixture using a rolling pin. Sprinkle sugar on top of the mixture as you are rolling it, to prevent the rolling pin from sticking.

cut out shapes Use the cookie cutters to cut out shapes from the coconut ice mixture. Place the shapes on a cookie sheet covered with baking parchment to dry.

finishing Sift confectioner's sugar over the coconut ice to create a pretty frosted effect. You may also wish to add other decorations, such as silver sugar balls. Coconut ice can be stored in an airtight container for about two weeks.

coconut ice

Deliciously sweet as well as irresistibly pretty,
coconut ice is fun and easy for kids to make,
and can be cut into decorative festive shapes.
This homemade version is truly delicious.

book bag

This pretty but practical wool book bag is decorated with a very simple festive Christmas tree motif formed from lengths of silver rickrack. It makes a lovely gift for a school friend or a younger family member.

YOU WILL NEED:

12in (30cm) wool fabric, 44in (137cm) wide • pinking shears • needle • white yarn • silver rickrack • scissors • glue • scraps of decorated white felt for pot and ball motifs

sew hem at top of bag Using pinking shears, cut a length of wool fabric measuring 22in (55cm) long by 10in (24cm) wide. Fold over the shorter ends by ½in (1cm) and work running stitch along this edge. The stitches should be approximately ½in (1cm) long.

continue sewing backwards When you have finished, start stitching backwards over the existing stitches, so there are no gaps. Repeat at the other end of the bag, then press the hems flat using a warm iron (it is advisable for an adult to do this).

stitch sides together Fold the piece of fabric in half widthwise with wrong sides together and stitch along the two side edges using the same stitching technique as used for the hem.

cut lengths of rickrack Cut nine lengths of silver rickrack braid to the following measurements: 6in (16cm), 5in (12cm), 4in (10cm), 3in (7cm), 2½in (6cm), 2in (5cm), 1½in (3.5cm), 1in (2.5cm), and ½in (1cm). Cut the ends on the diagonal to stop them fraying.

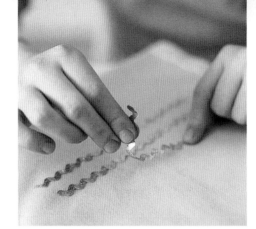

glue on rickrack Begin by applying a line of glue to the back of the longest length of rickrack. Carefully lay it on the fabric toward the bottom of the bag, about 3in (7cm) up from the base. Press flat using your fingers. Glue on the remaining lengths of rickrack in order of length, each about ¾in (2cm) apart, to form a Christmas tree shape.

glue on pot Cut out the pot shape and circular ball for the top of the tree from felt. Glue to the top and base of the tree shape and allow to dry completely.

make handles Cut two lengths of wool fabric measuring 13 by 2½in (33 by 6cm) for the handles. Fold one of the longer edges over by ¾in (2cm) then the other edge over the top of this by ½in (1cm) and press flat. Stitch down the center of each handle using running stitch and press with an iron (it is advisable for an adult to do this).

finishing Stitch one handle to the inside of the bag, working approximately 1½in (4cm) down from the opening and using neat whipping stitches to secure it in place. Repeat to attach the other handle to the other side of the bag.

pillow

We used pale green wool fabric to make this cute pillow decorated with a rickrack Christmas tree. This would work equally well in red wool fabric decorated with white or green rickrack. The pillow is made using a 12in (30cm) square of wool fabric and the back is made from two rectangles of wool, each measuring 7 by 12in (30 by 18cm) each, to allow for the back opening.

planted bulbs

Fragrant and decorative, planted bulbs are a welcome reminder that the warmer spring months lie ahead. They look very appealing in this painted terracotta pot tied with rickrack and felt decorations.

YOU WILL NEED:

**terracotta pot • silver paint •
paintbrush • scissors • double-
sided tape • red rickrack • felt
star decoration • flowering
bulbs of your choice •
potting mix**

paint pot Paint the flowerpot using
silver paint and leave it to dry. Paint the
inside of the pot from the rim to a depth
of about 1½in (4cm). If necessary, apply
a further coat of paint for better
coverage, then allow to dry completely.

tie on rickrack Cut a small square of double-sided tape
and stick it at the back of the pot on the rim. Fold the length of
rickrack in half to find the central point, then open it out and
attach the center of the rickrack to the piece of sticky tape.
Bring the ends to the front of the pot and tie in a bow.

add decoration Use scissors to trim the ends of the rickrack.
Using its hanging loop, tie the felt star decoration to the center of the
rickrack bow and firmly knot in position.

finishing Remove the bulbs from
their plastic pots and very carefully repot
them in the terracotta pot. You may
need to add some extra soil to the
bottom of the pot first. Gently push the
bulbs down into the pot and give them
a drink of water to finish.

YOU WILL NEED:

aluminum foil • 8in (20cm) square cake pan • ⅝ cup (140g) unsalted butter • 4 large eggs • ¾ cup (320g) superfine sugar • 1 tsp vanilla essence • ⅓ cup (75g) cocoa powder • ⅝ cup (140g) all-purpose flour • 3½oz (100g) milk chocolate • paper • confectioner's sugar

MAKES 16 BROWNIES

mix ingredients

Preheat the oven to 325°F (160°C). Cut a 10in (25cm) square of foil and use it to line the base and sides of the pan. Melt the butter in a saucepan over a low heat. Crack the eggs into a mixing bowl. Pour in the sugar, then add the vanilla. Stir well with a wooden spoon. Pour in the melted butter and stir. Set a sifter over the mixing bowl and sift the cocoa and flour onto the egg mixture. Stir well.

add chocolate

Break the chocolate into small chunks and add to the bowl. Stir until just mixed, then spoon the mixture into the foil-lined pan. Ask an adult to help you put the brownie mix into the oven. They will take about 40 minutes to cook in the center of the oven. To test if they are ready, push a cocktail stick into one, then pull it out. If the stick is clean, they are ready; if it's sticky, leave them for another 5 minutes.

cut out stencil

Ask an adult to remove the pan from the oven, as it will be very hot. Leave the pan to cool on a wire rack. When completely cold, remove the brownies from the pan, peel off the foil and cut into 16 squares. Trace the Christmas tree stencil on page 122 on paper and cut out the Christmas tree shape from the middle. This is your stencil.

finishing

Place the stencil on top of a chocolate brownie and sift confectioner's sugar over the stencil and brownie. Carefully remove the stencil to reveal the Christmas tree motif. Repeat until all the brownies are decorated.

chocolate brownies

These delicious chocolate brownies filled with chunks of chocolate are given a festive touch with stenciled Christmas-tree motifs made using sifted confectioner's sugar. If you can resist the temptation, they make great gifts for teachers, family, and friends.

YOU WILL NEED:

plain cake tin • red paint • paintbrush • assorted scraps of wrapping paper • scissors • glue • acrylic varnish (if desired)

paint tin Paint the tin inside and out using the red paint, then leave it to dry. If necessary, apply a further coat of paint for better coverage, then allow the tin to dry completely.

cut paper pieces Cut the wrapping paper into small squares and shapes using the designs of the paper as a guide. Experiment by laying the shapes on the top of the tin lid so you can figure out how many pieces of paper you will need.

découpage lid Start by sticking the pieces of paper to the corner of the lid. If the corners of the lid are curved, you will need to cut curved corners with scissors to fit. Continue to stick pieces of the paper all over the lid until the painted area is completely covered. Once the lid is finished, leave the glue to dry completely.

finishing When you have finished the lid, start sticking smaller motifs such as Christmas trees all the way around the sides of the tin. Leave the tin to dry completely. You may wish to apply a couple of coats of acrylic varnish to make the tin more hard-wearing. Allow to dry completely.

découpaged tin

Scraps of decorative wrapping paper glued
to a plain tin create a fantastic presentation
box for home-baked Christmas goodies
such as cakes, cookies, or brownies. Yum!

cards & wrapping

YOU WILL NEED:

**medium-sized potato •
star-shaped cookie cutter •
chopping board • sharp knife
(to be used by an adult only) •
paper towels or dry cloth •
paints in your chosen colors •
saucers to hold the paints •
sponge paint roller • plain
white paper**

cut out shape Cut the potato in half, making sure the surface of the potato is as flat as possible. Place the cookie cutter on a cutting board with the sharp edge facing upward. Press the potato firmly down onto the cutter, leaving the cookie cutter standing proud of the cut surface of the potato by about ¼in (5mm), so you can cut around it.

cut away edges Ask an adult to cut away the edges of the potato using a sharp knife. This needs to be done very carefully, to make sure the star shape is as clear as possible. Press the potato down on a dry cloth or paper towel to remove any excess moisture, which can make the paint watery.

apply paint Pour paint into a saucer and use the end of the sponge paint roller to apply the paint to the star shape. Don't apply too much paint to the potato, as this will make the design bleed. If you have applied too much paint, gently blot the potato on paper towels to remove the excess.

get printing Begin printing. To make sure the design prints clearly, use a gentle rocking motion, moving the potato from side to side without lifting it from the paper. This will apply the paint evenly, even if the cut surface of the potato is not flat. Continue to print the stars at evenly spaced intervals. Allow the paint to dry completely.

potato print wrapping paper

Potato printing is a traditional painting technique that is a favorite with kids of all ages. They can use cookie cutters to create pretty shapes, or an adult could use a sharp knife to cut out different shapes by hand.

stamped gift bag

Use a large potato and a tree-
shaped cookie cutter to decorate
a paper bag and a matching gift
tag to match. We used blobs
of glue sprinkled with silver
glitter to create the silver
bauble effect on the trees
and the pretty border along
the top edge of the bag.

holly cards

A holly leaf-shaped cookie cutter was used to create this festive design. It was then stamped onto plain bright–colored card to create funky Christmas cards. Decorated with dots of glue and silver glitter, the end result is both fun and festive.

little tips
Potato printing also looks very effective when carried out on fabric—but make sure you use fabric or stencil paint so the item can be washed. Follow the manufacturer's directions to set the fabric paint, as some fabric paints must be set with a hot iron.

stamped gift tags

These pretty gift tags are made using rubber stamps featuring decorative designs. You can make your own tags using a plain card, a hole punch and string ties. The stamped designs work equally well on gift cards and wrapping paper.

YOU WILL NEED:

card for tag • scissors • foam pad • stamping ink • rubber stamp • glue • hole punch • plain white paper • 6in (15cm) string per tag

cut out gift tag Cut out a rectangle of card measuring about 3 by 6in (8 by 15cm). Use scissors to snip off the top two corners of the card on the diagonal to form the top of the gift tag.

apply printing ink Cut out small pieces of white paper measuring about 2 by 3in (5 by 8cm). Using the foam pad, apply some stamping ink to the front of the stamp, making sure the design is completely and evenly covered.

stamp motif Place the stamp firmly on the center of a piece of white paper and use a gentle rocking motion to make sure that the design is completely transferred onto the paper. Leave to dry completely.

finishing Glue the paper design to the front of the tag. Use a hole punch to make a hole between the two angled corners of the tag. Thread the string through the hole in the tag to finish.

YOU WILL NEED:
paper • pencil • scissors •
blank cards • scraps of
wallpaper or decorative
wrapping paper for motifs •
pinking shears • glue

create template
Trace the star template on page 120 on a piece of plain paper and cut it out. Place the template on the back of the decorative paper, and draw around it. You will need two paper shapes per card.

cut out motifs
Use the pinking shears to carefully cut out the star motifs (you could use other decorative-edged scissors for different effects). See overleaf for more ideas for different festive motifs.

make center fold
Take one of the paper star motifs and fold in half, with the right side of the paper facing inward. Press down this fold. This is the 3-D element of the star on the front of the card.

finishing
Glue the unfolded star to the front of the card, making sure that all the corners are firmly stuck down. Now dab glue all the way down the fold on the back of the second star, and stick it on top of the first star. When the glue is dry, gently fold the corners outward to create a 3-D effect.

3-D christmas cards

Simple yet effective, these gorgeous 3-D cards can be made using scraps of decorative wallpaper or wrapping paper cut into festive shapes, then glued to plain cards.

gold and silver hearts

Using pinking shears to create a decorative effect, cut out small and medium-sized hearts from metallic wrapping paper. Glue the hearts onto gold and silver cards and finish with dainty bows made from gold ribbon.

blue bells

Simple bell shapes cut from blue and white paper create a pretty, punchy effect on plain white cards. They are topped with sheer white and blue ribbon bows to finish.

glittery trees

Sugar-pink and silver patterned wrapping paper looks very festive clipped into Christmas tree shapes. The trees are finished with "balls"—pale pink and silver sequins glued to the ends of the branches.

little tips

Instead of buying whole sheets of wrapping paper, visit a craft shop and buy a pack of craft paper. These packs include an assortment of decorative printed and embroidered papers that are the perfect size for making the cards here. Scraps of wallpaper also work well, as they are thicker than wrapping paper, which makes them ideal for 3-D shapes.

YOU WILL NEED:
round cookie cutter • felt
squares • pencil • scissors • 6in
(15cm) gingham ribbon, ¼in
(6mm) wide • glue • blank cards

cut out felt motif
Use the circular cookie cutter (or a similar object) as a template for the round shape on this card. Place it on the felt and draw aound it with a pencil. Carefully cut out the round shape. If you are making more than one card, it's a good idea to cut out all your felt shapes at the same time.

glue on hanging loop
Cut a piece of gingham ribbon about 2in (5cm) long and fold it into a loop. Glue the ribbon onto the card just below where the top of the ball will be positioned. Press down firmly to secure it in place.

stick on felt shape
Apply a thin layer of glue to the back of the felt ball shape and stick it on the card, making sure that you have covered both the ends of the ribbon loop. Press down firmly and allow to dry completely.

finishing
Make a ribbon bow from the gingham ribbon. Apply a small dab of glue to the back of the bow, and stick to the front of the bauble. Press down firmly to secure it in place and leave to dry completely.

felt motif cards

Felt is great for decorating cards since it comes in a wide selection of colors and does not fray once it is cut. We used Christmas-themed cookie cutters as templates for a variety of festive designs. Glue the felt shapes onto cardboard and finish them with dainty ribbon bows.

christmas trees

Christmas tree cookie cutters were used to cut out these shapes from plain red, white, and lime green felt. They were glued to cards, then decorated with tiny dots made using 3-D fabric pens.

glitter stars

Felt stars in plain and patterned felt adorn these square Christmas cards. We added a scattering of silver glitter glue dots for added decoration.

little tips

Some craft shops sell adhesive-backed felt, which is easier for younger children to use. Draw your chosen design on the backing paper, then cut it out with scissors. Peel off the backing paper, stick the felt to the greeting card, and decorate to finish.

YOU WILL NEED:
wrapping paper • stencil for motif • white paint • stencil brush • kitchen paper • double-sided tape • cardboard • hole punch • 16in (40cm) gingham ribbon, ½in (1cm) wide

fold paper Cut a piece of paper measuring 13 by 22in (56 by 33cm). Fold in 1½in (4cm) along one long edge, and 3in (7cm) along the other. Fold in the shorter ends by ¾in (1.5cm). Now fold the paper in half, so the shorter edges meet, and press flat. Open out, and on the wrong side of the paper, draw three lines, the first 5in (12cm) in from one short edge, again at 12in (30cm) and a final one at 15in (39cm). Fold the paper along each line. These folds form the box shape of the bag.

stencil motif Dip the brush in the paint and blot on paper towels to remove any excess paint. If there is too much paint on the brush, the outline will bleed. Hold the stencil over one of the larger panels of the bag (this will be the front) and dab on the paint. Let the paint dry slightly before removing the stencil.

fold side edge Open out the bottom fold of the bag, but keep the top 1½in (4cm) fold in place. Place some double-sided tape along one edge of the bag and press the other edge onto it to form a square bag shape. Press firmly down.

fold corners for base Open out the bag, turn it upside down and fold in the long sides to the middle. Fold the corners into triangles, and use double-sided tape to secure them. Cut a piece of card to fit the base and place it inside the bag to strengthen it. Punch two holes on the front and back of the bag just below the top edge and thread two 8in (20cm) lengths of ribbon through them. Knot the ends to hold them in place.

stenciled gift bag

What better than to present a handmade gift in your very own handcrafted gift bag? These were made from plain wrapping paper and stenciled with a Christmassy candy cane design.

templates

small heart for
center of
3-D card
(page 112)

heart for
3-D card
(page 112)

star for 3-D card
(pages 110–111)
and hanging felt stars
(pages 46–49)

(cut out center)

pompom disk
(pages 10–11)
cut two from cardboard

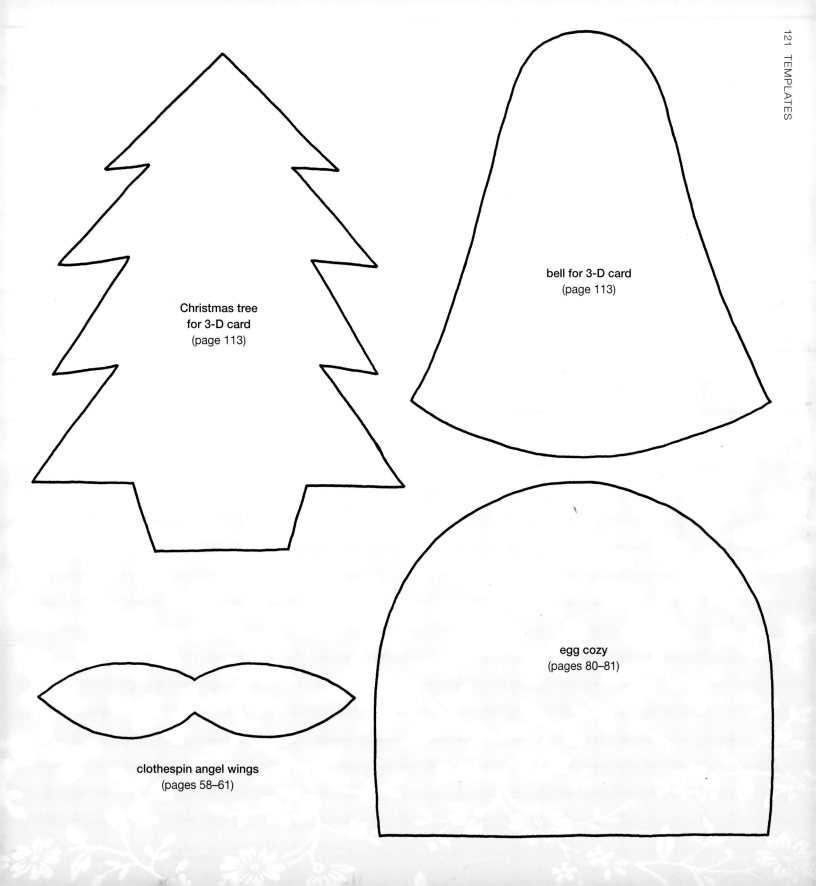

Christmas tree
for 3-D card
(page 113)

bell for 3-D card
(page 113)

egg cozy
(pages 80–81)

clothespin angel wings
(pages 58–61)

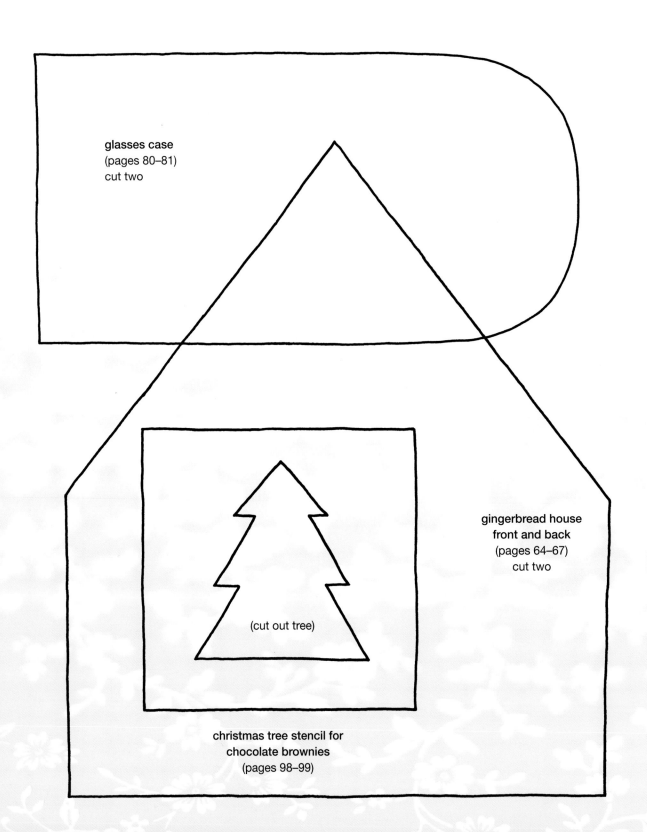

glasses case
(pages 80–81)
cut two

(cut out tree)

gingerbread house
front and back
(pages 64–67)
cut two

christmas tree stencil for
chocolate brownies
(pages 98–99)

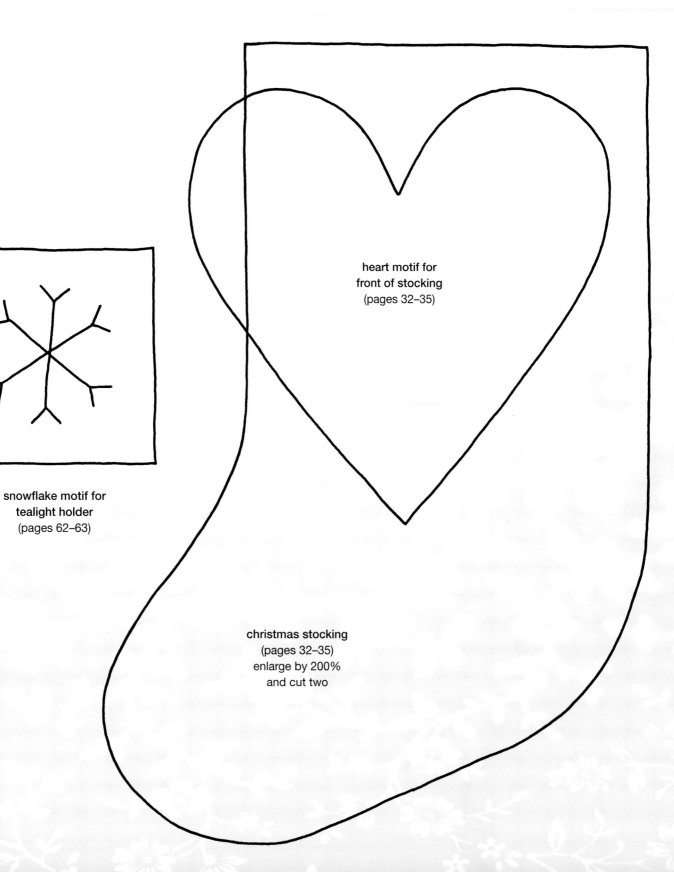

snowflake motif for
tealight holder
(pages 62–63)

heart motif for
front of stocking
(pages 32–35)

christmas stocking
(pages 32–35)
enlarge by 200%
and cut two

sources

A. C. MOORE
Call 866-342-8802 or visit www.acmoore.com for details of your nearest store. *Craft superstores carrying modeling clay, tealights, pipe cleaners, stencils, wooden clothespins, paper doilies, and natural wooden frames.*

THE BAKERS KITCHEN
3326 Glanzman Rd.
Toledo, Ohio 43614
419-381-9693
www.thebakerskitchen.com
Cake decorating, candy making, baking and kitchen supplies. Decorative doilies, baking cups, and a large range of cookie cutters in novel shapes.

DICKBLICK
Visit www.dickblick.com for details of your nearest store.

Cardmaking supplies, crepe, tissue, and decorative paper, stencils, ribbon, and more.

BRITEX FABRICS
146 Geary Street
San Francisco, CA 94108
415-392-2910
www.britexfabrics.com
Ribbons, trims, and notions.

THE BUTTON EMPORIUM & RIBBONRY
914 S.W. 11th Avenue
Portland, OR 97205
503-228-6372
www.buttonemporium.com
Vintage and assorted decorative buttons.

CANDYLAND CRAFTS
201 W. Main Street
Somerville, NJ 08876
908-685-0410
www.candylandcrafts.com
Baking and muffin cups, cookie cutters, edible cake decorations, fondant icing, piping gel, and sugar paste.

CHRISTMAS CRACKERS USA
www.christmas-crackers-usa.com
Ready-made party crackers, as well as components such as cracker snaps.

THE CRAFT PEDLARS
1009-D Shary Circle
Concord, CA 94518
877-PEDLARS
www.pedlars.com
Handmade paper and ribbon as well as a special section devoted to holiday crafting.

HEART OF THE HOME STENCILS
www.stencils4u.com
Alphabet stencils as well as other simple designs for kids.

HOBBY LOBBY
Locations nationwide.
Call 405-745-1100 or visit www.hobbylobby.com for details of your nearest store. *Arts and crafts stores.*

HYMAN HENDLER & SONS
67 West 38th Street
New York, NY 10018
212-840-8393
www.hymanhendler.com
Novelty and vintage ribbons.

IKEA
Call 800-254-IKEA or visit www.ikea.com for the location of your nearest store. *Unpainted wooden photo frames, plain tins for découpaging, and cute accessories.*

JAM PAPER
800-8010-JAM for your nearest store
www.jampaper.com
Paper, card, and envelopes of all sizes and customized rubber stamps.

JOANN FABRICS
Locations nationwide
Visit www.joann.com for details of your nearest store. *A wide selection of paper, card, fabric, scrapbooking materials, and more.*

KARI ME AWAY
www.karimeaway.com
Rickrack trim in a large variety of colors. Also cute novelty buttons different shapes, and glass beads.

KATE'S PAPERIE
561 Broadway
New York, NY 10012
212-941-9816
888-809-9880
www.katespaperie.com
Cute rubber stamps for kids.

LOOSE ENDS
2065 Madrona Ave SE
Salem, OR 97302
www.looseends.com
Paper for découpage, ribbon, ties, and trims, and more.

MICHAELS
Visit www.michaels.com for details of your nearest store. *Every kind of art and craft material, including beads, air-drying modeling clay, stamps, hole punches, ink pads, embellishments, glues, and natural wood frames.*

M&J TRIMMING
www.mjtrim.com
Fancy trims, including rhinestones, sequined flowers, ribbons, lace, rosettes, beaded braid, and fur and feather trims.

NEW YORK CAKE SUPPLIES
56 West 22nd Street
New York, NY 10010
800-942-2539
www.nycake.com
Comprehensive selection of bakeware, sugar paste, edible decorations, food colors, flavorings, ingredients, and cookie cutters in every shape.

PAPER CREATIONS
www.papercreations.com
Supplies for papercrafting and scrapbooking as well as rubber stamps.

PAPER SOURCE
1-888-PAPER-11
www.paper-source.com
Envelopes, blank cards, and handmade paper in a variety of designs, as well as crafting basics such as scissors, glue, and hole punches.

PAPER WISHES
888-300-3406
www.paperwishes.com
Paper, scrapbooks, stamping accessories, stickers, tools, and more.

PEARL ART AND CRAFTS SUPPLIES
Call 1-800-451-7327 or visit www.pearlpaint.com for details of your nearest store. *Brushes, modeling clay, adhesives, papers, and card.*

PRIZM
The Artist's Supply Store
5688 Mayfield Rd.
Cleveland, OH 44124
www.prizmart.com
Paints, paper, and more.

THE RIBBONERIE
191 Potrero Avenue
San Francisco, CA 94103
415-626-6184
www.theribbonerie.com
Extensive collection including wired, grosgrain, metallic, and velvet ribbons.

TARGET
Visit www.target.com for details of your nearest store. *Paper, scrapbooking accessories, tools, and more.*

TINSEL TRADING CO.
47 West 38th Street
New York, NY 10018
212-730-1030
www.tinseltrading.com
Vintage buttons and beads, as well as gorgeous silk and velvet flowers, sequins, metallic tassels, and exquisite ribbons.

THE ULTIMATE BAKER
1-866-285-COOK
www.cooksdream.com
Online cake-decorating supply store. Cookie cutters, food coloring, edible ink, and rolled fondant in many colors.

UTRECHT
Visit www.utrechtart.com for details of your nearest store. *Quality artists' materials and supplies. Modeling clay, natural wooden frames, paints, and craft paper.*

picture credits

ALL PHOTOGRAPHY BY POLLY WREFORD

Pages 2–3 air-drying clay, glitter, and ribbon from Hobbycraft, paintbrushes from The Wimbledon Sewing & Craft Superstore; pages 4–5 wool fabric, gingham, thread, and mother-of-pearl button from The Wimbledon Sewing & Craft Superstore; pages 6–7 air-drying clay, paint, spotted felt, and sequins all from Hobbycraft, wooden frame from IKEA, paper doilies, and blank greeting cards from Lakeland Ltd, rickrack from John Lewis; pages 8–9 silver card, yarn, pipe cleaners, and glitter all from The Wimbledon Sewing & Craft Superstore; mistletoe lights from a selection by Lakeland Ltd; pages 10–11 yarn, gingham ribbon, and 3-D fabric pen from The Wimbledon Sewing & Craft Superstore, white twigs from Lalage Barran Flowers; pages 12–13 yarn, felt, pipe cleaners, and 3-D fabric pens all from The Wimbledon Sewing & Craft Superstore, gingham ribbon from VV Rouleaux; pages 14–15 cinnamon sticks from Sainsbury's, gingham ribbon from VV Rouleaux, artificial Christmas tree from Bloom, bells from The Wimbledon Sewing & Craft Superstore; pages 16–17 white paper from Paperchase, bed linen from a selection at Cath Kidston; pages 18–19 oranges from Sainsbury's, gingham ribbon from VV Rouleaux, fresh Christmas tree from Lalage Barran Flowers; pages 20–21 artificial mini tree from a selection at Selfridges, candy canes from Lidl, gingham ribbons from VV Rouleaux, terracotta pot from Homebase, silver paint, sparkly pompoms, and silver ribbon all from The Wimbledon Sewing & Craft Superstore; pages 22–23 as above; pages 24–25 metallic wrapping paper from Paperchase, pink and silver sequined braid from The Wimbledon Sewing & Craft Superstore; pages 26–27 Fimo modeling clay and decorative gold dust from The Wimbledon Sewing & Craft Superstore; pages 28–29 as above; pages 30–31 glycerin from Sainsburys, distilled water available from pharmacies or hardware stores, Christmas figures, silver paint, brushes, and glitter all from The Wimbledon Sewing & Craft Superstore; pages 32–33 cream wool fabric, gingham, button, and embroidery thread all from The Wimbledon Sewing & Craft Superstore, red polka-dot felt from Hobbycraft; pages 34–35 as above; pages 36–37 silver card, yarn for pompom, glue, metallic pipe cleaners, and glitter all from The Wimbledon Sewing & Craft Superstore, artificial tree from Bloom; pages 38–39 as above; pages 40–41 metallic wrapping paper from Paperchase; pages 42–43 air-drying clay from Hobbycraft, cookie cutters from Jane Asher Party Cakes, glue, ribbon, and ribbons all from The Wimbledon Sewing & Craft Superstore, artificial tree from Bloom; pages 44–45 air-drying clay from Hobbycraft, paint, and sequins and sheer ribbon all from The Wimbledon Sewing & Craft Superstore, wrapping paper from Paperchase, colored string from a selection at IKEA; pages 46–47 felt and rickrack from The Wimbledon Sewing & Craft Superstore, mother-of-pearl buttons from John Lewis; pages 48–49 as above; pages 50–51 rocaille glass beads, wire, and silver ribbon all from The Wimbledon Sewing & Craft Superstore, silver wrapping paper from John Lewis; pages 52–53 silver and gold paint, glitter, bells, and ribbon all from The Wimbledon Sewing & Craft

Superstore; pages 54–55 wrapping paper from John Lewis; sequins and ribbons from The Wimbledon Sewing & Craft superstore; pages 56–57 as above; pages 58–59 paper doilies from Lakeland Ltd, silver card and metallic pipe cleaners from The Wimbledon Sewing & Craft Superstore, wooden clothespins from Hobbycraft; page 60–61 as above; pages 62–63 glass votives from IKEA; 3-D fabric pens from The Wimbledon Sewing & Craft Superstore, colored tealights from Homebase; pages 64–65 tubes of icing and ingredients from Sainsbury's, candy canes from Lidl; pages 66–67 as above; pages 68–69 florist's wire hoop and twigs from Lalage Barran, silver and gold paint and ribbons all from The Wimbledon Sewing & Craft Superstore; pages 70–71 craft papers from The Wimbledon Sewing & Craft Superstore; pages 72–73 ribbons and tissue paper from Hobbycraft; pages 74–75 as above; page 76–77 cellophane and air-drying clay from Hobbycraft, ribbon from VV Rouleaux, wrapping paper from a selection at IKEA; pages 78–79 terracotta pots from Homebase, silver paint and sheer ribbon from The Wimbledon Sewing & Craft Superstore, pillar candles from Colony; pages 80–81 felt from Hobbycraft; rickrack from a selection at IKEA, embroidery floss from The Wimbledon Sewing & Craft Superstore; pages 82–83 ready-rolled icing and cupcake cases from Jane Asher Party Cakes, tissue paper from Hobbycraft; pages 84–85 polka-dot felt from Hobbycraft; plain felt and embroidery floss from The Wimbledon Sewing & Craft Superstore; mother-of-pearl star-shaped buttons and egg cups from John Lewis; pages 86–87 red ribbon from The Wimbledon Sewing & Craft Superstore, cloves available from supermarkets and food stores; pages 88–89 ingredients available from supermarkets and food stores, tissue paper from Hobbycraft, decorations from a selection at Paperchase; pages 90–91 wool fabric and yarn from The Wimbledon Sewing & Craft Superstore, silver rickrack from Paperchase, silver/white felt from Hobbycraft; pages 92–93 green wool fabric from The Wimbledon Sewing & Craft Superstore, silver rickrack from Paperchase, silver/white felt from Hobbycraft; pages 94–95 terracotta pot from a selection at Homebase, red felt decoration from a selection at Paperchase, red rickrack and silver paint from The Wimbledon Sewing & Craft Superstore, bulbs from Lalage Barran; pages 96–97 ingredients available from supermarkets; pages 98–99 patterned découpage papers and paint from The Wimbledon Sewing & Craft Superstore, tissue paper from Hobbycraft, tin from Sainsbury's; pages 100–101 blank cards from Lakeland Ltd and Paperchase; patterned wrapping paper from Paperchase, felt from Hobbycraft; pages 102–103 cookie cutters from Jane Asher Party Cakes, sheer ribbons from Hobbycraft; pages 104–105 blank cards and bag from a selection at Paperchase, silver paint and glitter from The Wimbledon Sewing & Craft Superstore; pages 106–107 red card from Hobbycraft, stamp from The English Stamp Company; pages 108–109 blank cards from Hobbycraft, gingham wallpaper from Designers Guild; pages 110–111 blank cards and pink/silver wrapping paper from Paperchase, metallic gold and silver papers, ribbons, and sequins all from The Wimbledon Sewing & Craft Superstore; pages 112–113 blank cards from Paperchase, red polka-dot felt from Hobbycraft; pages 114–115 blank cards from Hobbycraft, felt and glitter from The Wimbledon Sewing & Craft Superstore; pages 116–117 wrapping paper from IKEA; stencil and red gingham ribbon from The Wimbledon Sewing & Craft Superstore.

index

3-D Christmas cards 110–11

A

angels
  angel tree topper 36–9
  clothespin angel 58–61

B

bags
  book bag 92-3
  stamped gift bag 106
  stenciled gift bag 118–19
beaded decorations 50–51
bells
  blue 113
  festive 52–3
blue bells 113
book bag 92–3
bulbs, planted 96–7
button photo frame 86–7

C

candle centerpiece 78–9
candy canes 20, 21, 119
cards
  3-D Christmas 110–11
  blue bells 113
  Christmas trees 116–17
  felt motif 114–15
  glitter stars 117
  glittery trees 113
  gold and silver hearts 112
  holly 107
chocolate brownies 98–9
Christmas cards, 3-D 110–11
Christmas crackers 54–7
Christmas stocking 30–35
cinnamon
  cookies 72–5
  sticks 14–15
clay decorations 42–5
clothespin dolls

angel 58–61
  Santa Claus 59
coconut ice 90–91
cookies, cinnamon 72–5
crackers, Christmas 54–7
cushion 94–5

D E

découpaged tin 100–101
egg cozy, felt 84–5

F

felt egg cozy 84–5
felt motif cards 114–15
festive bells 52–3

G H

gift tags
  stamped 108–9
  star 45
gingerbread house 64–7
glasses case 80–81
glitter stars 117
glittery trees 113
gold and silver hearts 112
hanging felt stars 46–9
holly cards 107

L M

lanterns, paper 24–5
mini tree 20–23

N O

nativity scene 26–9
orange pomanders 88–9
orange tree decorations
  18–19

P

paper lanterns 24–5
paper snowflakes 16–17
paper chains 40–41
peppermint creams 82–3
photo frame, button 86–7
planted bulbs 96–7
pomanders 88–9

pompom tree decorations
  10–13
  angel tree topper 36–9
  Santa Claus 13
  making pompoms 10
  miniature 20, 21, 22
  robin 13
  snowmen 12
potpourri 76–7
potato print wrapping paper
  104–5

R S

robin tree decoration 13
Rudolf the reindeer tree
  topper 39
Santa Claus
  peg doll 59
  tree decoration 13
  tree topper 39
scented gifts
  lavender-scented felt
    shapes 48
  tealight holders 62–3
snow globes 30–31
snowflakes, paper 16–17
snowmen
  peppermint creams 82–3
  tree decoration 12
sources 124–5
stamped gift bag 106
stamped gift tags 108–9
stars
  3-D Christmas cards
    110–11
  glitter 117
  hanging felt 46–9
  star gift tag 45
stenciled gift bag 118–19

T

tealight holders 62–3
templates 120–23
  bell for 3-D card 121
  Christmas stocking 123
  Christmas tree for 3-D

card 121
  Christmas tree stencil for
    chocolate brownies
    122
  clothespin angel wings
    121
  egg cozy 121
  gingerbread house 122
  glasses case 122
  heart for 3-D card 120
  heart motif for front of
    stocking 123
  pompom disc 120
  small heart for center of
    3-D card 120
  snowflake motif for
    tealight holder 123
  star for 3-D card and
    hanging felt stars 120
tin, découpaged 100–101
tree decorations
  beaded 50–51
  making pompoms 10
  miniature pompoms 20,
    21, 22
  orange 18–19
  robin 13
  Santa Claus 13
  snowmen 12
tree toppers
  angel 36–9
  gingham ribbon 22
  Rudolf the reindeer 39
  Santa Claus 39
trees
  Christmas 116–17
  glittery 113
  mini tree 20–23
twiggy wreath 68–9

W

wrapping paper, potato print
  104–5
wreath, twiggy 68–9

acknowledgments

Thank you to Polly Wreford for her beautiful photography and attention to detail in the wonderful pictures she shot for the book. Thanks to Toni Kay and Annabel Morgan for their help during all stages of the book—its design, layout, and words. Thank you to all the fantastic children who modeled for us—for their patience during photography, and their enthusiasm for the projects they worked on. Thanks to my daughters—to Jessica for designing and making the Nativity scene, and to Anna for helping to make some of the Nativity scene animals. Thanks are also due to Hobbycraft, for supplying their wonderful ribbons, card, and felt, and to The English Stamp Company for supplying the wooden stamps. Finally a big thank you to my husband Michael, for his unfailing support and encouragement.

Ryland Peters & Small would like to thank all the children who modeled for this book, including Aimee, Alessandra, Alissia, Amelia, Anna, Archie, Ayesha, Cameron, Chantal, Donnell-Andre, Hannah, Hassia, Honor, Jack, Jago, Jessica, Kai, Saskia, Tom, Tommy, and William.